TEXTS and STUDIES

OF

THE JEWISH THEOLOGICAL SEMINARY
OF AMERICA

VOL. XVII

STUDIES IN KOHELETH

THE STROOCK PUBLICATION FUND

*Established in Memory of Sol M. and Hilda W. Stroock and
Robert L. Stroock*

STUDIES IN KOHELETH

by

H. LOUIS GINSBERG

SABATO MORAIS PROFESSOR OF BIBLE

The Jewish Theological Seminary of America

NEW YORK

THE JEWISH THEOLOGICAL SEMINARY OF AMERICA

5711–1950

PRINTED IN THE UNITED STATES OF AMERICA
PRESS OF Maurice Jacobs INC.
224 N. 15th ST., PHILADELPHIA 2, PENNA.

TABLE OF CONTENTS

Foreword vii

I. Koheleth's Program 1

II. The Designation מלך as Applied to the Author 12

III. Koheleth Wrote in Aramaic 16

IV. Dates of Composition and Translation 40

Addendum to p. 35 45

FOREWORD

The connections and resemblances between this monograph and its bulkier predecessor with the similar title — *Studies in Daniel* (1948) — are more striking than the differences, but differences of course there are. One of the less obvious ones is that the present work makes easier reading than an equal quantity of matter from the other. That is so mainly because Koheleth itself is an easier, less complicated, book than Daniel. The hope that laymen may benefit directly by my researches is therefore perhaps a little more realistic this time.

Be that as it may, tho I would naturally make some minor changes in *Studies in Daniel* after the lapse of two years (as is indeed hinted in Study IV hereof), I am conscious of having served scholarship well therewith. May I feel even so two years hence about *Studies in Koheleth*.

It is again my pleasure to thank President Louis Finkelstein for including my studies in this Series.

H. L. G.

New York, September 1950.

I

KOHELETH'S PROGRAM

A. Bird's Eye View

1. Kọh 1:1 is of course the title of the book. The rest of Koh 1–2 is divided by most commentators into at least two units; by Galling into no fewer than seven. In my opinion, not only is Koh 1:2—2:26 a single unit, but it is a fitting introduction to the rest of the book.

2. Podechard has rightly seen that 1:3 is inseparable from 1:2 and that the two together state the subject of the book. But firstly, they also state more especially the subject of chs. 1–2;[1] secondly, in v. 3, as mostly in Koheleth, the verb *'āmal* means not 'to toil' but 'to gain or earn (by toil),' and the substantive *'āmāl* (as occasionally in talmudic Hebrew, Babylonian Aramaic, and Syriac, [Ps 128:2]) not 'toil' but 'gain, profit, or earning (thru toil), or yield, or income';[2] and thirdly, v. 3 is *not* a rhetorical question. The sense of vv. 2–3 is this: The world we live in is *heḇel*, or zero. This raises the practical question what *yiṯrōn*, or plus,

[1] Rashbam (Rabbi Samuel b. Meir, twelfth century, a grandson of Rashi), in his Commentary on Koheleth and Canticles, edited by A. Jellinek, Leipzig 1855, says on Koh 1:3: כל הדברים הללו מוסבים למטה על אין טוב באדם שיאכל ושתה וגו' [ב' כד–כו] לומר כל אלו מעשי האדם הבל הם ואין טוב מעשה להנאת האדם רק לשתות ולשמוח בחלקו. Apart from details, I had arrived at all of the conclusions embodied in this Study before I even learned of the existence of that rare little book. My attention was called to it by Prof. S. Lieberman, who was kind enough to read a first draft of this section of the monograph. — With the critical acumen that characterizes his better known commentary on the Pentateuch, our medieval rabbi and pietist attributes Koh 1:1–2 and 12:8–14 to the editors (pl.). I myself claim 1:2 and 12:8 for the author!

[2] Idem ad 2:24: בעמלו — ממונו אשר טרח בו. — In East Semitic, i. e. Accadian, *nēmēlu*, which is from the same root, means the same thing (and has *only* this sense), as is pointed out to me by Prof. Cyrus H. Gordon. See also n. 2a.

there can be for a man in the acquisition of worldly goods. But first the premise must be proved. This is done in vv. 4–11: the world is purposeless, therefore valueless.

3. Having thus introduced his theme, the author next introduces himself. He says in effect: "I was well qualified and most advantageously circumstanced for studying the world. Alas, I discovered that such inquiry is poor business, since the only discovery it leads to is that everything is *heḇel*, purposeless, and *r'ūṯ rūḥ*, useless (1:12–15). And that applies more especially to the two alleged purposes of life: the pursuit of wisdom (1:16–18) and the pursuit of pleasure (2:1–2)." Why it applies to the pursuit of wisdom Koheleth tells us then and there: On making a careful study of the merits of wisdom and knowledge versus madness and folly, he discovered that 'the greater the wisdom the greater the vexation, and the more knowledge the more grief.' For his devastating verdict upon the pursuit of pleasure, on the other hand, he doesn't deign to cite any arguments. It is not merely *heḇel*, or not positive, but *mhōlāl* 'mad,' or negative. The fact is that Koheleth loves wisdom and virtue (without excessive religiosity) and hates roistering, along with all other manner of fatuity (particularly the vocal varieties), and wickedness. For in the rest of the book too, he never mentions the two former but to praise them or else to explain why he is — reluctantly — compelled to discount their supposed advantages heavily, whereas he repeatedly condemns the two latter without apology. Better, he says among other things, a visit to a house of mourning — where one is at least profitably reminded of the transitoriness of life — than to a house of conviviality (7:2, 4). Even vexation, he avers, is better than frivolity — because the former may at least eventually result in happiness (7:3). Evidently, revelry and frivolity afforded Koheleth no gratification. The *śimḥā* which he so highly commends in other passages must be of a different sort. We shall presently see what it is.

4. From 2:3 (on the correct wording of which see B 2) to the end of the chapter Koheleth tells of his experiences while making the aforementioned study of wisdom versus folly, and how they furnished him with the answer to the question of 1:3. Thanks to his wisdom (v. 9b) he both gained many possessions (cf. vv. 19, 21) and had the sense to apply them to the satisfaction of his desires (cf. v. 26); which, he adds significantly, was the only good those possessions ever did him. To be sure, he had to admit to himself, upon reflection, that wisdom's superiority over folly is *sub specie aeternitatis*, and gains (which one ends by leaving to others) are *per se*, zero (*heḇel*), devoid of positive value (*yiṯrōn*); and he tells us why. Yet there remains in gain one potential purpose, or value, or plus, namely one's utilization of it for one's own enjoyment.[2a] This is not incompatible with the judgment pronounced in 2:1–2 on the pursuit of pleasure. For one thing, enjoying the earthly goods one acquires, tho it may mean very comfortable living if the goods are considerable, is not the same thing as idle and riotous living; which Koheleth, as we have observed, evidently abhorred as a matter of taste and temperament rather than of reason. And for another, as Koheleth is at pains to point out,

[2a] Here are Koheleth's exact words: '(2:18) So I took a dislike to my *'āmāl* which I am *'āmal*ing, because I shall leave it to somebody who will be after me . . . (24) There is nothing better for a man than to eat and to drink and gratify himself with his *'āmāl*.' And Ben Sira (14:14–15), no doubt echoing the foregoing, says, in his grandson's Greek version, this: 'Abstain not from the pleasure of the day, and let not a desirable morsel escape thee. Wilt thou not leave thy *ponoi* to another, and thy *kopoi* to sharers of an inheritance?' Surely there can be no doubt but (a) Koheleth's *'āmāl* and Ben Sira's *ponoi* and *kopoi* all mean 'gain, profit, substance, fortune,' and (b) *both* the Hebrew originals of *ponoi* and *kopoi* (not only one of them, as in our Hebrew Ben Sira) were words meaning literally 'labor(s).' In all probability, one of them was precisely our *'āmāl*. — Dr. Elias J. Bickerman calls my attention to the phrase *ex idiōn ponōn* (*kopōn*, *kamatōn*), meaning 'out of my (his, her, etc.) own resources or income'; which is of fairly frequent occurrence in the epigraphy of Syria (the sense of 'income' is particularly clear in Le Bas-Waddington, *Voyage archéologique en Grèce et en Asie Mineure* III no. 2412 1, and either 'resources' or 'income' ibid. no. 2037) and is surely an *Aramaism* for *ek tōn idiōn*, which is even commoner.

whether one does or does not enjoy one's gains depends (not upon oneself but) upon God's whim.

5. It is at 2:10, therefore, that we get the first intimation of what the answer to the basic question of 1:3 is going to be: in Koheleth's experience, the only *yiṯrōn* a man can have out of his *'āmāl* is applying it to his own enjoyment. The word used here, however, is not *yiṯrōn* but *ḥeleq* 'portion,' by which Koheleth means that which one can get out of one's gains, earnings, and acquisitions (*'āmāl* means all these things), and for that matter out of life; so also in 2:21; 3:22; 5:17, 18; 9:6, 9. Cf. further 8:15, where it is even possible that the difficult ילונו is nothing but a mutilated חלקו.

6. The practical conclusion from all these experiences of Koheleth is his answer to the question of 1:3, which is contained in 2:24–26. Since the superiority of wisdom over folly is subject to a qualification which renders it illusory, and since acquisitions *in themselves* are likewise an illusory asset, the only positive value is *the enjoyment of* one's gains. Unfortunately, even that is not given to everybody but only to those who are pleasing to God; to those who are not, He gives nothing but an obsession with making gains for the others to enjoy — which is a *heḇel* and a *r'ūṯ rūḥ* if ever there were any! That God likes just the righteous and dislikes just the wicked is in no way implied.

7. I have named Koh 1:2—2:26 Koheleth's Program. The following chapters consist largely of further demonstrations that wisdom and acquisitions are at best vanity (*heḇel*, *r'ūṯ rūḥ*), and that acquisitions can even be a grievous ill (*rā'ā ḥōlā*, *ḥlī ra'*), or minus, followed by variations of the conclusion of the Program (2:24–26) to the effect that a man gets the only good, advantage, portion (*ṭōb*, *yiṯrōn*, *ḥeleq*) or plus, he ever can get out of life when — *Deo volente*! — he enjoys what he acquires. These variations of

the original conclusion are 3:12–15; 3:22; 5:17–19; 9:7–10;[3] while 11:8—12:7 is a grand finale in the same vein and is followed by 12:8, which is practically identical with the beginning of the book (1:2) and obviously marks its end. The last six verses don't purport to be by Koheleth. (11:9b and 12:1a are either interpolated or don't mean what they seem to.[4])

8. In stressing the importance of enjoying one's goods oneself, Koheleth has occasion to polemize a number of times against the belief in immortality (3:18–21; 9:4, 10; 11:8). In stressing the worthlessness of wealth in itself, he has occasion to polemize against restless laboring to amass, out of sheer competitiveness, more wealth than one can ever use (4:4–8) and against failing to use the wealth one has (5:12–6:9). Inevitably one asks oneself

[3] Cf. the stereotyped conclusion of the chapters, which are both numbered and titled, of the Insinger papyrus: "The fortune and fate which come are decreed by the deity." I translate after the rendering of Aksel Volten, *Das demotische Weisheitsbuch*, 1941. It was doubtless because he was unable to utilize this work, which is based on a comparison of the Insinger papyrus with parallels to parts of it contained in four fragments in the Carlsberg Museum, Copenhagen, that Galling, tho he quotes the above formula on p. 59 of his commentary on Koheleth (1940), failed to realize its full significance, or that of the Demotic ethical work as a whole for Koheleth. Not only Koh 2:24–26 but the variations cited above are parallel to the Insinger refrain; in as much as what we have in Koheleth is also a refrain, albeit one whose wording is freely varied instead of being rigidly fixed. See also n. 5.

[4] The Talmud, of course, discovers in 11:9b a double-entendre (one will be called to account for every pleasure one has *missed*), and this Levy believes to be actually intended. However, the half-verse is more probably an interpolation from the hand of the last epilogist; cf. 12:14. — In 12:1 *bwr'(y)k* may mean simply 'thy vigor,' from a (probably segolate) substantive *bore'* corresponding to post-biblical *borī* 'health' (see the Talmud lexica); cf. Ehrlich. (Or rather, the Aramaic original had (*br'k* or) *bryk*, by which the author intended (*bor'āḵ* or) *boryāḵ* 'thy vigor' but which the translator understood as (*bār'āḵ* or) *bāryāḵ* 'thy Creator'; see Zimmermann, *JQR* 36 [1945]: 32.) Torczyner, *Hal-Lashon wehas-Sefer* I, 1948, p. 467, likewise interprets *bwr'(y)k* as 'thy *bore'*,' but takes this word to mean 'plentiful feeding' (cf. 1 Sam 2:29). — Nevertheless, 11:10 *aa* means 'drive *discontent* from your flesh'; cf. B 2 ii. (Not 'sickness,' as claimed by Zimmermann, *JQR* 40 [1949]; 90 n. 10. The original doubtless had באישה, but the translator rendered it correctly.)

whether these motifs in any way reflect the age he lived in; see below, Study IV. But in any case, they are there.

9. Of course those were not the only thoughts he ever had. I have already hinted that he was a man of tastes as well as of purely intellectual convictions. One can be ever so disillusioned about the practical or ultimate value of wisdom and virtue in mortals ruled by fate and doomed to oblivion, and yet have decided preferences for wise men over fools, for honest men over knaves, for diligent ones over sluggards, for temperate ones over sots, for good rulers over bad, and so on. Koheleth has, and he sometimes digresses from his main theme to express them in very conventional-sounding gnomes (7:1 ff.; ch. 10). He also has views on, e. g., certain aspects of religion and — rather loosely — works them in too (4:17—5:6). But his main theme is nevertheless the one set out in his Program.[5]

B. Philological Detalis

1. Ad 1:1, 12, 16; 2:7, 9. See II. [Ad 2:7, 9. See pp. 25–26.]

2. Ad 2:1–3.

(i) It must be emphasized that *'ē zē* (v. 3) can never mean 'what,' either as a primary or as a secondary (to employ Jespersen's convenient terms). It means either 'where' as in 1 Sam 9:18; Isa 50:1; 66:1 etc. — cf. *'ē mizzē* 'whence,' Gen 16:8 etc. — or 'which' as in Koh 11:6. 'What,' whether used alone or with a substantive (='what sort of'), is *mā*. Omitting examples of the former usage as superfluous, compare for the latter Gen 37:26;

[5] The affinities that can be discovered between Koheleth and the Insinger papyrus (edited by F. Lexa, 1926) with the aid of the acute literary analysis and partial new translation of the latter by Volten go far beyond the single example given above in n. 3. A study of these affinities can be dispensed with here, but not in any commentary on Koheleth, or in any study of his literary and intellectual relationships, which may be undertaken henceforth.

1 Sam 26:18; Isa 40:18; Jer 2:5; Mal 3:14; Ps 30:10 (see also Mal 1:13). It is no different in Koheleth — see 1:3; 5:10, 15 — or in talmudic Hebrew: שכינה מה לשון אומרת (Mishnah Sanh. 6:5) 'What expression does the Shekinah employ?'; מה קול שמעת בחורבה (TB Berakot 3a) 'What sort of voice did you hear in the ruin?' Accordingly not only coherence but grammar is served by Torczyner's removal from our verse, Koh 2:3, of the words ביין את בשרי ולבי נהג,[6] which leaves us free to interpret the remainder as follows: 'I resolved in my heart to grasp (lit. 'tug at') wisdom and hold on to folly (cf. 7:18), to the end that I might discover which was good for men to practice etc.' When, moreover, it is considered that three of the five words in question pertain unmistakably to the riotous living in which, as we have seen (A 3), Koheleth recognizes no positive element, whereas our verse begins his account of the experiment which taught him the only positive thing in life (A 4–6), one can not but admire the instinct which led Torczyner (now Tur-Sinai) not only to excise the offending phrase from v. 3 but to transfer it precisely to v. 1, which relates Koheleth's wholly negative experience with pleasure-seeking.

(ii) He also actually determined its exact original position, namely after the word אנסכה in v. 1. However, it must be admitted that if the latter is awkward in the Masoretic Text ('I said *in* my heart, Come now, I will try *thee*[7] [or, I will pour a libation] with merriment'), inserting the five words from v. 3 after it makes the entire sentence even more awkward — unless אנסכה is emended to אית(י)בה.[8] But surely the sense which results when that is done is precisely what Koheleth intended: 'I said in my heart, Come

[6] See Torczyner in *Vom Alten Testament Karl Marti zum siebzigsten Geburtstage gewidmet*, 1925, pp. 279 f.

[7] This rendering assumes a spelling of the suffix meaning 'thee' which is rare in MT generally and particularly strange for the MT of Koheleth.

[8] For אנסכה miswritten for אית(י)בה cf. Cant. 2:17; 4:6 (read with three ancient verions ונטו; cf. my *Studies in Daniel*, p. 78 n. 19); Ps 4:7 (read נְטֵה; cf. Gen 39:21).

now, I will gladden my flesh[9] with wine, my heart engaging in merry making and experiencing (vocalize *wrō'ē*) enjoyment.' That with reference to the heart and the face "good = contented, glad; bad = discontented, sad" is well known; cf. 7:3; 9:7; 11:9–10, and numerous passages in other books (e. g. Jud 19:22; Esth 1:10).

(iii) With the offending five words removed from v. 3, there is no mention of enjoyment in the account of Koheleth's decisive experiment until v. 8, or really 10. V. 3 states that Koheleth tested wisdom versus folly, and vv. 4–7 that he acquired a tremendous amount of *'āmāl*. Indeed, I believe most students will decide on closer inspection that v. 8 also comes under the heading of *'āmāl* 'acquisitions,' and that v. 9 says, "All those things I acquired in the way of wordly goods with the help of my wisdom" (cf. vv. 19, 21). Only then does v. 10 say: "And I didn't hesitate to spend of this wealth on personal enjoyment." Thus it is even clearer than before that the enjoyment Koheleth approves of is different from the "pleasure" of 2:1–2; 7:2 (*mištē*, conventionally rendered by 'feast,' really means 'drinking-party'); 10:16, 19. He believed in enjoying life, but he simply didn't enjoy vulgar pleasures. One suspects that he also disliked idleness for himself as well as for others (cf. 11:4, 6). His ideal was partaking of one's *earnings* (*'āmāl*).

3. Ad 2:12. Here another text-critical operation, namely Galling's transposition of 12a and 12b, is unavoidable; in as much as (a) vv. 12a, 13–17 make a perfect, coherent paragraph, which is ruined by the intervention of 12b between 12a and 13–17, and (b) even as the Masoretes construed 12b it makes far better sense as a justification of v. 11 than as a justification of v. 12a. However, as the Masoretes understood it, it is not a perfect sequent even

[9] As in 11:10, 'flesh' seems to be synonymous with 'heart.' Cf. further 5:1, 5: A man's mouth saddles his 'heart' with an obligation by uttering a vow; it will bring down displeasure upon his 'flesh' if he fails to keep the vow. (For לחטיא 'to render . . . displeasing,' cf. v. 3 and below para. 6.) See further Ps 16:9; 84:3.

to v. 11, and that is why I here part company with Galling. Within 12b, instead of changing consonants in order to obtain nothing better than a smoother wording for the sense which the Masoretes found in this half-verse, it is possible to obtain a perfect sequent to v. 11 by a mere change of vowels. In vv. 18–19 the author states that he was filled with distaste for all the things he was acquiring under the sun by the thought that there was no knowing what the אדם שיהיה אחרי . . . וישלט בכל עמלי שעמלתי ושחכמתי 'the man who will be there after me . . . and have at his disposal all of my earnings which I have earned by toil and wisdom' might be like. The sense of vv. 11, 12b is the same: the author concluded that all of his acquisitions were *heḇel* and *r'ūṯ rūḥ* and devoid of *yiṯrōn* because מה האדם שיבוא[10]אחרַי הַמֹּלֵךְ את אשר כבר עשוהו 'of what sort will be the man who will come after me, who will reign over that which has already been achieved?' That this comes close to the sense intended by the author will hardly be doubted. Of course if anybody feels that it is necessary to change המלך 'who will reign' to וימלך 'and will reign,' that is graphically permissible.[11] But it is really only the end of the half-verse that still doesn't sound quite right, especially in the Hebrew. In the light of v. 11a, it is conceivable that עשוהו in v. 12b is miswritten either for עשוהו ידי (by a sort of haplography) or, better, for עשו ידי. In that case the concluding relative clause is to be rendered by 'that which has already been achieved by my hands.' Still better, of course, would be עשיתי: 'that which I have already achieved.' — The force of the verb *mlk* in v. 12b is in any case vouched for by that of its synonym *šlṭ* in the parallel v. 19;[12] and moreover, *mlk*

[10] This change already in Podechard's commentary (1912), tho he does not transpose the clauses and otherwise interprets divergently.

[11] The emendation is even slighter in the original Aramaic: די מלך (who rules) to די ימלך (who will rule).

[12] Cf. the frequent *juridical* use of the participle of this verb and of its derivative *šallīṭ(ā)* in the Elephantine papyri (='having the disposal, ownership, of').

in Arabic means precisely 'to own, or gain possession of' and governs the accusative ot the thing owned, just as in Koh 1:12b as vocalized above. See further Study II.

4. Koh 2:18–19, however, is not merely parallel to but the continuation of vv. 11, 12b; whether one actually shifts this verse and a half beyond v. 17 (as I prefer to do) or not. For observe the structure of the paragraph 2:12a, 13–17. Here the report on the author's negative finding on wisdom (12a, 13–16), introduced by 'I considered' (*up̄ānīṯī 'nī*), is followed by a statement about his resulting chagrin (v. 17) introduced by 'So I was disgusted with' (*wśānēṯī*). So too vv. 11, 12b, introduced by 'I considered' (*up̄ānīṯī 'nī*), report his negative finding on material acquisitions, and vv. 18–23, introduced by 'So I was disgusted with' (*wśānēṯī 'nī*), the chagrin resulting from this.

5. Ad 2:16b. Read בשכרב (*bšekkrōḇ*), possibly בשברב (*bšebbrōḇ*): 'For as the succeeding days multiply, everything is forgotten'; cf. 11:1b.

6. In conclusion a few notes on 2:24–26. The expression *ṭōḇ lip̄nē* in v. 26 is an Aramaism (see Dan 3:32; 6:2) for the more Hebraic *ṭōḇ b'ēnē* 'to be pleasing to,' just as its antonym *ra' 'al* (2:17) is an Aramaism (see Dan 6:15) for *ra' b'ēnē* 'to be displeasing to.' For 'one who is displeasing to God,' however, Koheleth doesn't say *ra'* at all but *ḥōṭē*, that is to say 'one who falls short, fails, misses, or loses'; see especially Isa 65:20b*b* ('he who fails to attain the age of one hundred years shall be deemed accursed'); Prov 8:36 ('but he who loses, or fails to find, me,' contrasted with 'he who finds me' in the preceding verse); Job 5:24b ('when you visit your abode you will miss nothing'). When the same verb (tho in the hiphil conjugation according to the masoretic vocalization) was used of missing a target (Jud 20:16), it in reality meant to the native speech-instinct 'to fail to find or attain' just as in the three foregoing examples, since in Hebrew hitting a mark is finding it (1 Sam 31:3). That *ṭōḇ* and *ḥōṭē* imply no moral evaluation in

Koh 2:26 and 7:26 is now generally recognized. I suggest that the same holds good for 9:2b*b* and 9:18 (unless we read in the latter *ḥeṭ* — with the sense of 'error,' however, and without any moral connotation). I also wonder whether 7:20 does not conceal the sense 'For there is no righteous man in the world who becomes (vocalizing *yē'āśē*) pleasing and does not displease,' or 'who fares well (3:12) and does not fail.' (Does this verse properly follow 7:16?)[13] — For the rest, it is well known that in 2:24 a *mem* has dropped out at the beginning of the fourth word by haplography, so that the sense (cf. especially 3:22) is 'There is nothing better for a man than that he eat and drink etc.' V. 25 might be read thus: כי מי יאכל ומי יְחָשַׁח חוץ [14]ממנו, and rendered thus: 'For who partakes, and who uses,[15] except by His doing?'[16] (Cf. 6:2.)

[13] See further above, n. 9.

[14] So with some manuscripts and ancient versions.

[15] Aram. *ḥšḥ* (Dan 3:16; Ezr 6:9; 7:20), if correctly emended. (I assume that the final *ḥ* of *yḥšḥ* has been lost thru haplography before *ḥwṣ*, and that a *w* has crept in after the first *ḥ* of the former thru contamination with the sequence *ḥw* of the latter.) See C. Brockelmann, *Lexicon Syriacum*[2], 1928, pp. 261b–262a; and compare especially, in the Peshitta version of Ben Sira 30:19 (*Libri Veteris Testamenti Apocryphi* e recognitione Pauli Antonii de Lagarde, 1861, p. 31), מן דאית לה עותרא ולא מתחשח בה 'one who has wealth and doesn't use it.'

[16] But actually, the Aramaic original probably read something like this: די מן י(ה)וכל ומן י(ה)חשח בר מנה 'For who causes to partake or to use but He?'

II

THE DESIGNATION מלך AS APPLIED TO THE AUTHOR

1. With 2:12b eliminated (above, I B 3), there remain two passages in which the author is apparently represented as a king: 1:1 and 1:12. In the former he is designated as 'the Convoker,[1] the son of David, a king in Jerusalem.' That is a remarkable bit of prosopography for the following reasons: (1) It gives the author two vocations — convoker and king — and not a single real name. (2) It apparently does not realize that 'the Convoker' is an appellative indicating a calling, and not a proper name. (3) For post-Canaanite times, even 'king *of* Jerusalem' would be astonishing (it is never used, despite the constitutional distinctness of Jerusalem from Judah). (4) '(A) king *in* Jerusalem,' implying that there could be more than one at a time, is simply amazing. The Septuagint and daughter-versions have, it is true, 'king of Israel in Jerusalem.' But firstly, if that had been the original reading nobody would have thought of altering it to that of the Masoretic Text and of the remaining versions deliberately; while an accidental loss of ישראל (thru haplography) before בירושלם, which does not resemble it very closely (note the initial ב), can not very well have occurred in the very first verse. And secondly, the reading of MT in 1:1 is supported by the testimony of all the witnesses in 1:16 and 2:7, 9. In 1:16[2] the Convoker boasts that he acquired more wis-

[1] There is no doubt about that being the *meaning* of (*haq-*)*qōheleṯ* (the form with the article in 12:8 and [*textu emendato*] 7:27), and that is what matters here. The *form* will be explained, with the help of the translation hypothesis, in Study III, para. 12.

[2] For על ירושלם read בירושלם (contamination by על of the preceding phrase).

dom, and in 2:7, 9 that he acquired more wealth, 'than all that were before me *in Jerusalem.*' These observations raise the question whether 'over Israel' has not been interpolated in 1:12 just like 'of Israel' in LXX et filiae's text of 1:1, and for the same reason: the strange protocol 'a king in Jerusalem.' I believe it has been, and that 1:12, like 1:1, originally described the author of our book simply as מלך בירושלם.

2. That being so, one inevitably asks further whether that phrase really has the curious sense of 'a *king* in Jerusalem.' I suggest that it has not, at least in 1:12. The Convoker tells us only of his intellectual and economic pursuits; and while neither are incompatible with royalty, an account of *res gestae* in which the author introduces himself as a king but relates absolutely no achievement, undertaking, or activity of a specifically royal character — such as waging war, erecting public buildings, administering justice, governing the people, or even observing them incognito — is passing strange. (2:8 implies nothing more than that Koheleth acquired treasures *such as* kings do.) Puzzling is also the comparison with 'all that were before me etc.,' instead of 'all *the kings* that were before me' or 'every *king*' (see the *res gestae* of Azitawanda, Kilammuwa, Bir-Rekub, etc.). And what king, or self-styled king, would ever have related that 'I saw all the oppression that went on' (4:1) but to add that he put an end to it thruout his realm? See further 5:7. And why does the epilog (12:9) evidently know nothing about the Convoker's kingship?

3. It has been suggested,[3] mainly on the basis of a half-jesting usage of Babylonian amoras, that 'king' in this connection means 'sage,' or even 'head of a school.' However, the danger of anachronism in this solution is obvious, and the book of Koheleth itself suggests a different one. We have seen (1 B 3) that in 2:12b המלך is to be vocalized הַמֹּלֵךְ and rendered 'who will possess.'

[3] See Levy, pp. 34–5.

Similarly in our 1:12 (from which, as explained above, על ישראל is to be deleted) מלך is to be vocalized מֹלֵךְ and rendered 'a man of means, or a property-holder.' This is very naturally followed by 'in Jerusalem'; cf. מהחסן ביב בירתא 'property-holder in the fortress of Elephantine' in descriptions of parties to contracts from Elephantine.[4] Of course, Koheleth's purpose in telling us that he was a property-holder or a man of means is not to acquaint us with his vocation — that purpose is served by the word *Koheleth*, which is notoriously not a proper name (tho I shall continue to employ it as one faute de mieux) but an appellative meaning 'the Convoker,[5] — but merely to explain how he was in a position to do the things he is going to tell us about. That is why he says 'I, the Convoker, *was* a man of property in Jerusalem'; that he still is is irrelevant. In Arabic, by the way, the difference between 'king' (*malik*) and 'possessor' (*mālik*) is exactly one mora.[6]

[4] A. Cowley, *Aramaic Papyri of the Fifth Century B. C.*, nos. 7:2; 8:2 (cf. 3:3; 33:6).

[5] In the words of the *Leqaḥ ṭob* of Tobiah b. Eliezer (eleventh century) — made famous by Barton's delightful mistranslation of them (p. 67) — קהלת שהיה מקהיל קהלות ודורש ברבים 'Koheleth (was his soubriquet) because he used to call crowds together and preach in public' — like Socrates.

[6] Another possible example of *mōlēḵ* 'propertied (person)' occurs in 10:20 (מלך // עשיר). — In still another passage, the sense 'to own' has been proposed for *mlk* before now, but unfortunately it does not solve every difficulty there. According to Torczyner (now Tur-Sinai) — נ. ה. טורטשינר [טור־סיני], שיר השירים, 1943, p. 23 above — (who of course likewise invokes the Arabic *malaka*), Koh 5:8 means 'And the advantage in land above all is to own (מְלֹךְ, cf. Arab.) a field that is tilled.' This interpretation attributes to *'ereṣ* a sense which in Hebrew is proper to *'ḏāmā*; tho that could be due to the influence of Aram. *'ra'/'ar'ā*, which has both the senses of the English 'land.' It also leaves 'above all' (בכל) something of a problem. But otherwise, if by 'tilled' we understand 'tilled by tenants' our sentence follows well on the preceding verse, with which it is connected by 'and': Provinces are oppressed for the ultimate benefit of the king; and tenant-farmers — who are sometimes not even lessees but sub-lessees — toil for the ultimate benefit of the landlord. On the other hand, Tur-Sinai's attempt to connect our verse with the following instead of the preceding (a) disregards the copula at the beginning of our verse, (b) smuggles in a 'but' at the beginning of the next one, and (c) otherwise subjects the latter to a forced exegesis.

4. Thus originally the body did not any more than the epilog claim for the author either the social rank or the antiquity of Solomon. The superscription probably did, even supposing that it did not originally include the phrase 'son of David.' For it is in any case secondary in relation to the body of the book (whose true opening is 1:2, identical with its true closing 12:8), since it evidently misunderstands 1:12 to imply that Koheleth is the speaker's actual name and only מלך his vocation.

III

KOHELETH WROTE IN ARAMAIC[1]

1. In Study I, I deliberately segregated the philological details, because my thesis as to what constitutes Koheleth's program stands independently of emendations and details of exegesis. Similarly I separated I and II because each can stand entirely on its own merits, and only I B 3 and II receive considerable confirmation from (but are by no means dependent upon) each other. I further relegated to footnotes[2] my four incidental references in I and II to the Aramaic original from which I believe our Koheleth to have flowed, because my reasoning thruout Studies I and II does not rest even partly upon the translation hypothesis. Critics with lucid minds and unatrophied consciences will recognize these mutual independences, and will not obfuscate issues by urging non-sequitur conclusions as to the soundness of I A from real or imaginary weaknesses in I B, II, or the present study; or as to the soundness of I B from real or imaginary weaknesses in I A, II, or the present study; or as to the soundness of II from real or imaginary weak-

[1] Note the following papers and their sigla: F. C. Burkitt, *JTS* 23 (1922): 22–28 (=Burkitt); A. Fernández, *Biblica* 3 (1922): 45–50 (=Fernández); F. Zimmermann, Aramaic Origin of Qoheleth (summary of paper read at Annual Meeting of the Society of Biblical Literature and Exegesis, Dec. 28, 1944), *JBL* 64 (1945): vii (=AOQ); Idem, The Aramaic Provenance of Qohelet, *JQR* 36 (1945): 17–45 (=APQ); Idem, The Question of Hebrew in Qohelet, *JQR* 40 (1949): 79–102 (=QHQ); C. C. Torrey, *JQR* 39 (1948): 151–60 (=Torrey); R. Gordis, The Wisdom of Koheleth, With a New Translation, *The Menorah Journal*, Summer 1943, pp. 147–173 (also published as a book, New York 1945) (=*WK*); Idem, The Original Language of Qohelet, *JQR* 37 (1946): 67–84 (=OLQ); Idem, The Translation-Theory of Qohelet Re-examined, *JQR* 40 (1949): 103–116 (=TTQR); H. L. Ginsberg, *Studies in Daniel*, 1948 (=*SD*).

[2] I nn. 4, 11, 16; II n. 1.

nesses in I or in the present study; or as to the soundness of the present study from real or imaginary weaknesses in the preceding.

2. For nearly five years after Zimmermann enunciated his hypothesis of an Aramaic original of Koheleth,[2a] my impression was that neither he nor his critic had proved his case. However, the most recent, simultaneous, broadsides from both battleships, which happened to be fired at the end of a twelvemonth period during which I had, on and off, given the book of Koheleth some thought (the fruits whereof be Study I herein), aroused me to examine the translation theory carefully; with the result that I was converted to it.

3. In the case of Daniel, I was "converted" before I had ever heard of Dr. Zimmermann.[3] That I was able to remain skeptical for so long after he had propounded his theory about Koheleth is no doubt partly due to the fact that the Hebrew of Koheleth is less outlandish than that of Dan 8–12. If, however, Koheleth can nevertheless be shown to contain, like Dan 8–12, mistranslations from Aramaic such as can only with difficulty or not at all be conceived of as due to the author,[4] the superiority of its flavor over

[2a] I. e., Dec. 28, 1944. See n. 1.

[3] I presented my thesis orally to an Annual Meeting of the American Oriental Society five months before his first article was published; see *JAOS* 58 (1938): 540.

[4] As I have explained in *JBL* 68 (1949): 405–6, a mistranslation which can not stem from the author himself is one which renders a foreign expression other than the one the author had in mind. Applied to Koheleth that means that, for example, it would be barely conceivable that an author thinking in Aramaic and writing in Hebrew would render his native מטל די (*miṭṭol dī*) by מצל אשר and that the latter would be corrupted to כצל אשר by a scribe who was misled by the proximity of the word 'days' in Koh 6:12 and 8:13 (see below para. 9 iii); but only a translator other than the author could have rendered an Aramaic *bṭol* and *bṭullaṯ*, meaning 'in the shadow of,' where the author himself had in mind *bṭel* and *biṭlaṯ* 'it has ceased,' (see below para. 8 iv). Moreover, that translator could only have so mistaken the author's intention if he *read* him; since it is the Aramaic *graphemes* for 'it ceased' and 'in the shadow of' that are identical (i. e. בטל[ת]), whereas the spoken Aramaic expressions, as we have seen, are quite distinct. With the aid of this example, the intelligent reader will be able to decide for himself which of the mistranslations cited in the following pages could pos-

that of Dan 8–12 is no counter-argument, and is easily accounted for by the greater intelligibility of the content — the very circumstance which accounts for the superiority of the translation in Dan 1:1—2:4a over that in chs. 8–12. As it is, neither Dan 1:1—2:4a nor Koheleth is wanting in inelegance or Aramaic coloration; and whereas the former, thanks to its brevity, perhaps contains only one mistranslation,[5] the latter contains not a few.

4. As in his articles on Daniel, not all of Zimmermann's arguments are cogent. I have already taken exception to some,[6] and I shall have occasion to reject or qualify others in the course of the following discussion. But after every legitimate objection has been raised, enough remains of Zimmermann's pleading to establish his case.

5. In the first place, the cumulative force of the enormous proportion of Aramaisms (APQ A) and the utterly erratic use of the article (APQ B) *is* decisive. In connection with the former, I may note in particular that a satisfactory alternative to Zimmermann's explanation of יהוא (11:3) as a purely Aramaic form (corresponding to Hebrew יהיה)[7] retained in the Hebrew translation has *not* been offered: something similar will be suggested below, in paras. 13 and 14. In connection with the article, it may be remarked that while in 9:9 the absence of the article is compatible with good sense and good grammar (regardless of whether Koheleth was or was not a bachelor, 'a woman [wife or otherwise] thou lovest' makes excellent sense), and while Zimmermann's criticism may not

sibly be perpetrated by an author and which only by a translator. The intelligent reader will also realize that the presence of a few specimens of the latter category proves that those of the former are in fact (whatever they theoretically might be by themselves) likewise errors by a translator who is not identical with the author.

[5] In Dan 2:1; see *SD* 59.

[6] I B 5 is by implication a criticism of APQ 39. See further Study I n. 4 end.

[7] This is on a par with תנתן (*tintin*) for Hebrew תתן in Dan 8:12, see *SD* p. 50; המלך (*hamlik̲*) for Hebrew מלך (*mālak̲*) in Dan 9:1, ibid. pp. 59–60; and the Aramaic preformative *y*– in *ya'modnā*, Dan 8:22b, ibid. p. 56 top.

be well founded in one or more further cases, attempting to explain away the majority of cases of improper prefixing or omission of the article is precisely the sort of thing the Talmud (TB Baba Meṣi'a 38b) deprecates as 'forcing an elephant into a needle's eye.'[8]

6. To be sure, I do not agree with Zimmermann that the sloppiness of the translator in the use of the article is due to a recession of the absolute state in the dialect of the Aramaic original. The case of the Hebrew of Daniel, where we know the dialect of the original (from the Aramaic portions of that book), proves that a person who translates from an Aramaic which retains all the niceties in the use of the *states* into a language with a *prepositive article* is liable to blunder hopelessly in the use and non-use of that article.[9] Similarly the Septuagint again and again omits a necessary article in cases where the Hebrew expresses determination by means of the construct state (which means the form which governs pronominal suffixes as well as other nouns) instead of the article; e. g., Koh 9:3, *kardia huiōn tou anthrōpou . . . en kardiāi autōn en zōēi autōn*; outside Koheleth, cf. Hos 1:1–3; 4:11–12; Zeph 1:8; 2:8; Jer 2:2a; 11:2 (*pros andras Iouda*); 20:4 (*en makhairāi ekhthrōn autōn . . . eis kheiras basileōs Babulōnos*), etc. It should be noted that in about fifty per cent of cases the Hebrew construct state actually differs *consonantally* from the absolute (i. e. in the singular of nouns with feminine ending and in the plural of nouns with masculine ending); but the Septuagint translators had not been taught that "the construct state can not take the article, which must be supplied in Greek if the sense requires it," nor indeed did they know either of the terms in question (tho the Greek *gram-*

[8] In this connection it is necessary to correct the notion of TTQR 110 that '*b̲īd̲ā* in Aramaic can only be the passive *participle* singular (masc. emph. or fem. absol.) of the verb '*b̲ad̲*. Torrey had in mind the singular absolute of a *substantive*, meaning 'labor' and the like, which can be traced from the Elephantine papyri (Cowley 9:10; 21:6; Aḥiqar 21, 127, 208) down to the Talmuds and Targum Onqelos (here often spelled עיבידא, emphatic עיבידתא).

[9] Cf. *SD* 80–81 n. 17.

marians had a word for 'article'). Septuagint translators are naturally even more erratic in the use of the article when they translate from Aramaic, which not only shares with Hebrew the construct state (hence the Greek translator's omission of several articles in Ezra 7:20, for example) but employs a third (the emphatic, or determinate) state in lieu of the Hebrew article. No wonder the Greek translator of Ezra 6:3, in an unwary moment, could render the emphatic state of the Aramaic word for house by *oikos* (without the article) and the absolute state of the Aramaic word for 'sacrifices' by *ta thusiasmata* (i. e. with the article). And no wonder that against such errors the Hebrew translator of the Aramaic Koheleth — which doubtless employed the states as correctly as the Aramaic portions of Ezra and Daniel — was not proof either. But, all apologetics notwithstanding, the manner in which the article is inserted and omitted in the Hebrew of Daniel and Koheleth would be most wondrous if the Hebrew were original.

7. Again, under the heading of "Exegetical" (APQ H), Zimmermann makes at least one observation which is striking. Surely his explanation of 'downward to the earth' (למטה לארץ) in 3:21 as a dual rendering of an Aramaic לארע 'downward' (// 'upward' [Heb. למעלה <Aram. לעל]) is the best yet.

8. Furthermore, some of Zimmermann's examples of mistranslation (APQ C) and of confusion of הוּא (or הָוֵא) and הוָא (APQ D) are telling.

(i) In 7:5 'praise' is so vastly more appropriate than 'song' that it must be assumed to have been the sense intended by the author if it is at all possible to explain plausibly why, in that case, the text has *šīr* 'song.' That *šīr* "could have" secondarily acquired the sense of 'praise' — note that the Aramaic *šbḥ* went thru the opposite development — could only claim consideration as a hypothesis if either (a) other instances of *šīr* with this sense could be adduced or (b) no other hypothesis were available. But no other instance of *šīr* 'praise' is known, while an excellent other hypothesis is available. For the Hebrew of this verse is immediately accounted for by the hypothesis that the book of Koheleth is a translation from Aramaic. In Aramaic (including Syriac) several substantives from the root *šbḥ* not only "could have been" but are employed in the two senses of 'song' and 'praise,' just as the verb *šabbaḥ* in *that* language not only "could have meant" but does mean both 'to praise' and 'to sing.'

(ii) Of course, it has been argued that even if *šīr* is not correct Hebrew for 'praise,' it may nevertheless be Koheleth's Hebrew (OLQ 72); and while in my experience not even poor linguists whose native speech is German have perpetrated in original composition such delectable howlers as "chief hair" (<*haupthaar*) for "hair of the head," or "news (reports)" (<*kunden*) for "customers," or "a cabbage (<*kraut*) with long roots" for "a *plant* etc." (whereas all three of these boners exist black on white in *translations* — including a translation by a brilliant linguist — the German originals of which are likewise extant), all this would theoretically be possible. However, the theory of an author writing down in Hebrew what he thought in Aramaic is untenable in Koheleth for another reason, the very same one that precludes it in Daniel: namely, that the translator's errors are not confined to inept renderings of the author's Aramaic, but extend to renderings of Aramaic expressions other than those intended by the author.[10] Take for example 10:17. Here the author and the translator can not be the same person, since the former had had in mind Aramaic *ḥausān* (so Syriac) or *ḥōsān* (חוסן) 'moderation' (from the verb *ḥws* 'to spare') where the translator rendered Aramaic *ḥsen* (חסן) or *ḥson* (חס(ו)ן) 'strength.'[11]

(iii) The Hebrew of the last clause in 12:13 can only mean 'for

[10] Cf. above n. 4.

[11] I have already pointed out in para. 6 that there is no reason to doubt that the Aramaic original of Koheleth used the absolute state wherever the rules of official and western Aramaic require it.

that is the whole man.' That does not follow coherently upon the preceding clauses, nor does v. 14 follow coherently upon it. On the other hand a relative clause meaning 'who judges every man' would fit the context perfectly (for the position of the relative clause cf. Jonah 1:9). The Aramaic for that is די דָאֵן (דָיֵן) כל אנש, which a translator could very well mistranslate into what the Hebrew offers if he read דאן (or דין) as *ḏēn* instead of *ḏā'en* (or *ḏāyen*). So Zimmermann. I myself prefer to assume that the Aramaic original was די ידין כל אנש 'who will judge every man,' (cf. the tense of v. 14) because the translator would be more likely to mistake די ידין for די דין (haplography) than דאן (which is more likely to have been the spelling of the participle of *dyn* than דין, in view of the spelling of the participles of hollow verbs in the Aramaic of Daniel and Ezra) for ד(י)ן. But either way, the verse is mistranslated, and the translator can not be identical with the author because he translates a different Aramaic word from the one the author had in mind.

(iv) So too in 7:12 בצל (twice) shows that the translator thought *bṭol* (בטל) and **bṭullaṯ* (בטלת) 'in the shadow of' where the author had thought of *bṭel* (בטל) and *biṭlaṯ* (בטלת) '(it) has ceased.' The author's complete phrase was evidently בטלת חכמתא בטל כספא, the proper sense of which is 'when the wisdom goes, the money goes too.' It has been objected that a conjunction meaning 'when' or 'if' would be necessary. That is not so. Cf. (TB Baba Batra 16b) אידלי יומא אידלי קצירא 'when the sun rises, the patient arises (=gets well)'; (Genesis Rabbah XLVIII, on Gen 18:8) עלת לקרתא הלך בנימוסה 'when you enter a town, follow its custom';[12] or in Hebrew: (TB Erubin 15a) נכנס יין יצא סוד 'when wine goes in, discretion goes out';[13] (Mishnah Abot 5:19) בטל דבר בטלה אהבה 'when the motive passes, the love passes too.' The resemblance of

[12] '(When) in Rome do as the Romans do.'
[13] 'When the wine is in the wit is out.'

the last quotation to the above restoration of Koh 7:12a is sure to strike everyone. — The restoration is of course Zimmermann's: I have merely taken the liberty of changing his participles to perfects (a) because of the analogy of the foregoing parallels, and (b) because בטלת is more likely to have been mistaken for the *construct state* of a substantive than בטלה(א). I am, however, in a position to add that the two other occurrences of 'shadow' in Koheleth are likewise mistranslations of the consonant group טל in the original Aramaic; see below.

(v) One can only feel sorry for anybody who, after reading Zimmermann APQ D, is still satisfied with Koh 3:15 as it stands, or even with the explanation that the interchange of הוא and היה here and elsewhere is due to miscopying of the Hebrew rather than mistranslation of the ambiguous Aramaic graph הוא. I go even further than Zimmermann and consider the second היה a mistranslation too. It ought to be הוּא or הֹוֶה (cf. 2:22): 'Whatever is (הוּא or הֹוֶה) already has been (היה), and whatever is to be already is (הוּא or הֹוֶה).' That, as Zimmermann asserts, the Aramaic original's הוא ought also to have been interpreted as הוּא (=Heb. הוּא) instead of הֲוָא (=Heb. היה) in 4:16; 6:10; 7:10 seems to me at least probable. At any rate, I am able to add two striking instances of Aram. הוא -*hwā* mistaken for הוא -*hū*, and a probable one for the contrary error; see below.

(vi) I have already cited Zimmermann's attractive explanation of the mysterious 'creator' (it *is* mysterious, even tho we shall doubtless be assured that it makes excellent sense in the context) in 12:1.[13a]

I do not wish to leave this review of Zimmermann's more cogent proofs without mentioning two more points:

(vii) The suggestion that הרבה in 5:6 and רבים in 7:29 represent Aramaic שׂגין, equivalent to English 'people err' in the first instance

[13a] Study I n. 4.

and to 'erroneous' in the second but mistaken for שׂגין 'many' in both, deserves at least serious consideration.

(viii) The suggestion that in 10:15 עמל הכסילים תיגענו goes back to טרחותא די שטיא תשלהנה, with the third word read שְׁטַיָּא instead of שָׁטְיָא by the translator, at least affords a plausible explanation of the extraordinary syntax of the Hebrew. An analogy would be the rendering of ודרעין מנה יקומון by וזרועים ממנו יעמדו instead of by וזרועות ממנו תעמדנה in Dan 11:31,[14] and something similar from Koheleth itself will be cited immediately hereafter. Consequently one ought not to be deterred by a priori arguments about the limits of translators' stupidity (about which it will be necessary to say some plain words at the end of this study) from adopting Zimmermann's reconstruction tentatively.

(ix) That הכל לפניהם הכל (9:1–2) goes back to כְּלָא קדמיהון כַּלָּא, 'all is as naught before them,' may also be.[15]

9. Of my own contributions to this problem, I shall begin with those to which I have had occasion to refer above in connection with Zimmermann's, and shall continue with those which deal with difficulties which Zimmermann has sensed in some degree but has in my opinion either not defined quite correctly or not solved quite correctly or completely. After that I shall make some observations which do not come under either of these headings.

(i) *Ad* para. 8 viii. The plural of *pardēs* does not occur in the Bible outside of Koh 2:5. Here it takes the plural ending *–īm*. But the numerous post-biblical passages have *pardēsōṯ* except in

[14] See *SD* 48.

[15] Here may also be mentioned Burkitt's observation on 7:14. The final phrase certainly means, in accordance with Syriac idiom, precisely 'man may find no fault with Him.' Since post-biblical Hebrew employs the similar phrase *hirher 'aḥar* rather frequently in the sense of 'to criticise, blame,' one might be willing to accept Koheleth's unique expression as a Hebrew author's Aramaism; were it not introduced, into the bargain, by the conjunction *'al diḇraṯ še–* (on which see Dan 2:30; 4:14 and below, para. 9 iii), and if not for the considerations pointed out above in n. 4.

the phrase *gannōṯ u-pardēsīm*, which is borrowed from our verse, and they sometimes substitute the ending *–ōṯ* even there.[16] By itself this would hardly prove anything, but in the light of the foregoing and the following it is exceedingly probable that the form *pardēsīm* owes its existence solely to the circumstance that our verse is translated from Aramaic. The Aramaic *pardēsīn* was rendered by a "Hebrew" *pardēsīm* (instead of *pardēsōṯ*) in exactly the same way as the Aramaic *šabbū'īn* was rendered by a "Hebrew" *šāḇū'īm* (instead of *šāḇū'oṯ*) in Dan 9:24 and the Aramaic *drā'īn* by a "Hebrew" *zrō'īm* (instead of *zrō'ōṯ*, the dual *zrō'aim* being inapposite in the sense in question) in Dan 11:31. [That the translator of Koh 2:5, who was led by his Aramaic archetype into giving *pardēs* the plural ending *–īn*, was nevertheless not led into doing the same thing for the plural of *gannā* may indicate that his Aramaic archetype had the rarer Aramaic plural *gannān* instead of the commoner *gannīn*, but not necessarily. In phenomena of this sort, inconsistency is the rule. Thus the man who let the Aramaic *drā'īn* mislead him into coining *zrō'īm* at Dan 11:31 had remembered the conventional Hebrew *zrō'ōṯ* at v. 15.]

(ii) *Ad* para. 8 v.

(a) The Hebrew of the last three words of Koh 1:5 is difficult to defend. The absence of a relative particle would be strange for Koheleth under any circumstances, and even in ancient poetry it would be strange before a participle, as would also the use of participles (instead of imperfects) with reference to daily occurrences. Harsh is also the order participle-third person pronoun where neither the participle nor the third person pronoun is emphatic: the latter ought either to be dispensed with altogether (as with *šō'ēp*) or to precede the participle. Zimmermann's reconstruction of the Aramaic original of our relative clause is, however, impossible. Firstly, because the difficulty of the postpositive *hū*

[16] See the references in I. Löw, *RÉJ* 89 (1930): 150–1.

is as acute for Aramaic as for Hebrew; and secondly, because the participle of the verb *nwḥ* is, in Aramaic, not *nāḥ* but *nā'aḥ* (or *nāyaḥ*). I have a strong feeling that the original was (די) דנח הֲוָא תמה 'where it rose,' די having been lost thru haplography. I only hesitate between the vocalizations *ḏānaḥ* and *ḏnaḥ* for דנח. At least in Syriac, the latter (which would make [*h*]*wā* a mere expletive) is as possible as the former. That the Hebrew הוא represents a misunderstood Aramaic הֲוָא seems almost certain. — In this connection I should like to add a suggestion on v. 5b*a*. Zimmermann's hypothesis (APQ 23–24) that *šw'p* represents an Aramaic *t'b* is somewhat difficult. It would be rather strange if a writer who thought that *t'b* (i. e. *tā'eḇ*) meant '(it) desires' rendered it by the Hebrew verb *š'p*; in as much as the latter, a cognate of *š'b* 'to draw (water)' — Arab. *s'b* 'to drink' — means simply 'to swallow, inhale, gasp (for), pant (for).' Perhaps it is possible, after all, to understand our *šw'p* in the sense that the Targum did, namely that of 'it glides.' The verb *šwp* 'to glide,' common in Babylonian Aramaic (corresponding to Palestinian Aram. *šḥp*) is employed in Hebrew in Genesis Rabbah I 6 precisely with reference to the motion of the sun. Even on this interpretation, however, the form *šō'ēp̄* (instead of *šāp̄*, as in the cited passage in Genesis Rabbah, which is formed according to the rule for participles of hollow verbs) would be due to the analogy of the Aramaic participle *šā'ep̄* (cf. the participles of hollow verbs in Dan 2:38; 7:16) and would be most naturally explained as a thoughtless translation of the latter. I further suggest that מקומו is a mistranslation of אתרה, which was taken as *'aṯreh* 'its place' instead of *'aṯrā* 'the place.' Koh 1:5b will then have read in the original Aramaic ואל אתרה(א) שאף (תאב?) די דנח הֲוָא תמה, of which a correct rendering would have been ושף (ושב?) אל המקום אשר זורח היה שם (or זרח).

(b) Even if it should be denied, הוא in Koh 9:15 is troublesome. The rule is that with a finite verb the pronominal subject is only added for emphasis. (In the first person, the emphasis is a little difficult to sense, notably in Koheleth; but that doesn't affect our הוא, which is third person.) Yet here it is not the subject but the verb that is emphatic (not '*he* would have saved the city,' but 'he would have *saved* the city'). What is required is either ומלט without הוא or, better, וממלט היה < ומשיזב הוָא. (וישיזב הוָא may also be considered, since ונשוזב הוָא would probably be proper in Syriac; cf. above para. a on Koh 1:5.) Thus the ambiguous Aramaic graph הוא has again been misunderstood by the translator. [Of course the verb in the original may have been the pael of פלט, rather than the one which occurred to me first. But the הוא of our verse would still represent a misunderstood Aramaic הוא (=hwā).]

(c) I strongly suspect that the first clause in 12:9 read in the Aramaic something like ויתיר די הוא קָהֲלָא חכימא עוד אלף מנדע לעמא 'To be added: That the said wise Convoker further taught knowledge to the people'; *Hebraice*: ויתר שהמקהיל החכם ההוא עוד למד דעת את העם. For the construction cf. הוא צלמא 'the said image,' Dan 2:32. No epilogist would have supposed (as ours did according to the received Hebrew text) that the average reader who had gone thru the book needed to be assured that its author was a sage, or that such an assurance would have done any good to one who still needed it at that stage. Besides, note the absence of 'and' (ו) before 'further' (עוד). — For evidence that the Aramaic original of (ה)ק(ו)הלת was קָהֲלָא see below para. 12.

(iii) *Ad* para. 8 iv. No less than a quarter of a century ago, Torczyner[16a] sensed that כצל אשר, Koh 6:12; 8:13 must mean exactly the same thing as בשל אשר in 8:17, namely 'because.' At that time it was reasonable to conclude that the former was a purely scribal corruption of the latter (particularly since the LXX and two of its daughters interpret the first letter as ב). But meanwhile Zimmermann has made his observations on Koheleth, and

[16a] Loc. cit. (See Study I n. 6.)

more particularly the one discussed above in para. 8 iv. In the light of the latter, Torczyner's observation on כצל אשר must be reformulated as follows:

Even as כל עמת ש־ (5:15) is a translation of כל קבל די,[17]
as על דברת ש־ (7:14) is a translation of על דברת די,
and as בשל אשר (8:17) is a translation of בדיל די,
even so ומ׳צל אשר (6:12; 8:13) is a translation of מְטֵל די.

Whoever wishes to is welcome to make all the capital he likes of the כ which this explanation assumes to have supplanted an original מ either in the Aramaic original or in the Hebrew translation. The fact remains that the two could easily have been confused in the script of, for example, some of the Khirbet Qumrān ('Ain Fashkha) manuscripts; especially by a copyist or translator whom the reference to a man's short 'days' which immediately precedes in both 6:12 and 8:13 had misled into thinking that the 'shadow' was a figure for the brevity of man's life as in Ps 144:4, Job 8:9[18] (which, however, make sense), and especially since מ *by itself* (i. e. contracted from the common מן) very rarely serves as a preposition in any but Babylonian Aramaic (e. g. in Syriac only in half a dozen combinations, including our *meṭṭol*).[19] Of course, some exegetical

[17] That כל עמת, if it were native Hebrew, would be descended from an original *כְּלְעמת (cf. TTQR 107) is true, but does not prove that it is not borrowed from an original כל קבל; since the latter is certainly descended from an original *כְּלְקֳבֵל. See Gesenius-Buhl s. v. קֳבֵל, where the later Aramaic כְּלַפֵּי (<*כְּלְאַפֵּי) — which by the way was notoriously borrowed outright by talmudic Hebrew — is rightly compared.

[18] Also 1 Chr 29:15.

That many a כי in our Koheleth represents an original מטל די whose translation, thanks to the absence of a distracting 'days' in its neighborhood, was not bungled by the translator is very possible indeed.

[19] The possibility that this preposition may mean etymologically 'from the shadow of' was considered, among others, half a century ago by C. Levias, *A Grammar of the Aramaic Idiom of the Babylonian Talmud*, 1900, p. 51. It has in its favor the common spelling of *meṭṭol* without a vowel-letter in Syriac, which is most naturally explained (like the *scriptio defectiva* of *kol*) as a carry-over from the time before the Syrians took to expressing *short* u/o by means of the vowel-

acrobats may argue that the comparison of man's days with a shadow was precisely what Koheleth wished to express in the two passages in question, but again they are welcome to. Alternatively, opponents of the translation hypothesis may argue that all four of the remarkable conjunctions listed above are merely *adapted* from the Aramaic, and by themselves they barely possibly might be; but they can not be in the light of those cases where the translator has not given a poor Hebrew rendering of the author's Aramaic expression but rendered a totally different Aramaic expression. We have already had a number of such cases, including one where the translator's Aramaic contained our word 'shadow' but the author's Aramaic didn't (above, para. 8 iv). Below are some more of the same type.

10. Zimmermann rightly sensed that there was a certain lack of "crispness" in Koh 8:8, and that it was due to mistranslation. His mistake was that he sought the trouble in the word *mišlaḥaṯ*. The latter serves in Ps 78:49 as a noun of action to the piel of *šlḥ* in its sense of 'to send out (against), let loose (upon)'; and there is no reason why it should not serve here as a noun of action to the same verb in its sense of 'to release, set free,' since it is parallel to the piel of *mlṭ*, meaning 'to deliver, rescue.' For the major pause in Koh 8:8 is not, as the masoretic accentuation implies, immediately after but immediately before v. 8a*c*. That being so, the problem in v. 8a*c* is rather the word *milḥāmā* 'war.' Not only, as Zimmermann has observed, is it not true that there is no release for the individual in war, but — what is even more important — it is equally untrue that there is no escape for the individual from death in war; yet it is of death that every one of the four clauses of Koh 8:8 speaks. The first two speak of its inevitability: 'man is not master over the spirit to restrain the spirit (from leaving the

letter waw. (Long u/o had been so represented since the sixth century.) The word *ṭol* 'shade' is also spelled *defective* in TP Rosh hash-Shanah II 58b top.

body), and there is no mastery over the day of death'; the last two speak of its finality: 'neither is there any release in the . . ., nor can . . . deliver its owner.' For our purpose it doesn't matter much whether we read in the second blank space 'wickedness' in accordance with the Masoretic Text or 'riches' in accordance with the plausibe emendation עשר (*'ošer*). In the first blank space, however, the word desiderated by the context is clearly 'grave' (in the sense of 'nether world,' Ps 88:12); but just as in the sentence 'קבר(י)ם (='graves') or קברימו (='their graves') are their houses for ever, etc.' (Ps 49:12) the first word, somewhere along the line of transmission, got garbled to קרבם 'their inside,' so in the Aramaic original of the clause just quoted, 'neither is there any release בקברא (=in the grave),' Koh 8:8, the last word became corrupted to (or was misread by the Hebrew translator as) בקרבא 'in war.' Is there any other *plausible* explanation of the Hebrew במלחמה?

11. Similarly in Koh 5:5, if the 'messenger' were really the sense intended there would be absolutely nothing the matter with המלאך. It is not true, as Zimmermann implies, that מלאך has in *biblical* Hebrew the specific nuance of 'angel.' It is, on the contrary, the commonest word for a messenger of any kind (so also in Ugaritic), and is of course rendered by 'messenger' in the English Versions except when the reference is to a supernatural agent of YHWH. The trouble with המלאך in Koh 5:5 is rather that just the sense of 'messenger' is — apart from exegetical difficulties — linguistically improper after the expression 'to say *before* (i. e. in the presence of).' The preposition 'before (in the presence of)' instead of 'to' after verbs of saying is reserved for the Deity (cf. Koh 5:1a) and for kings (cf. Dan 2:10, 11, etc.) and satraps.[20] Those Ancient Versions which render as if the text had האלהים (as in v. 1a) follow a true instinct, but such a reading can not be the origin of the masoretic one. To me it seems that there must

[20] See A. Cowley, *Aramaic Papyri of the Fifth Century B. C.*, no. 32, ll. 2–3.

have been in the Aramaic original from which our Hebrew text was translated a situation analogous to that which obtains in Jer 2:17b*b*–18a*a* (and elsewhere); where a phrase is written twice, once incorrectly and once correctly (no doubt as a result of some scribe mechanically copying both a correction and the blurred or corrupt phrase which the correction had been meant to supersede). That is to say, the Aramaic may have read ואל תאמר קדמוהי {די שליחא} די שלו היא; in which די שלו היא had originally been intended as a correction of, not as an addition to, the matter I have enclosed in braces. The sense of the original, correct, Aramaic text will then have been simply 'And say not before Him (referring to God, v. 3), It is an error.' (די introduces a direct discourse, as in Dan 2:25 and in countless parallels in Syriac and Greek.)

12. Zimmermann's acute observation, that the peculiar form of the Hebrew *(haq)qōhelet̠* — which is that of a *feminine* participle active of the qal, with, in two passages (12:8 and 7:27, where read אמר הקהלת), the *article* added — reflects an Aramaic *masculine* participle active of the peal with the *emphatic* ending *–ā* (written ה or א), and that the latter was in all instances mistaken for the outwardly identical feminine ending and in the aforementioned two instances both so mistaken *and* correctly identified, is at once brilliant and correct. Zimmermann, however, assumed that the Aramaic participle in question was כְּנָשָׁה; whereas I think I can persuade him, among others, that it was קָהְלָה(א).

The one argument in favor of כנשה as against a homologous derivative of another root is Zimmermann's observation that it is isopsephic with שלמה 'Solomon.' But firstly, the designation 'the Convoker' is the author's own (note 1:12 in particular), whereas the identification of the Convoker with Solomon is secondary. (See above, Study II.) And secondly, isopsephism (Hebrew גימטריה < γεωμετρία) is out of the question in our book. The use of the letters of the alphabet as numeral signs is an Ionic invention which did not spread even to all of the Greeks until the Hellenistic age, and which so far as I know makes its appearance in Semitic writing for the first time on coins of the First Jewish Revolt (66–70 C. E.); where, since ש stands for שנה 'year,' א = '(year) 1,' שב = 'year 2,' שג = 'year 3,' שד = 'year 4,' and שה = 'year 5.'[21] The Old Semitic numeral signs are attested among the Jews for only a few decades earlier.[22] That disposes of pre-Christian *gemaṭriot* among them. Yet they were among the first Semites to borrow the use of letters as figures. On Phoenician coins of the Hellenistic period, the legends in the native idiom express numbers only by means of the old West Semitic numeral signs;[23] which Palmyrenes continued to

[21] For the final proof that the coins in question date from the First Revolt see E. L. Sukenik, *Kedem* 1 (1942): 12–19. As Prof. Saul Lieberman has explained to me, it is because the Semitic aleph, unlike the Greek alpha, has not yet acquired the sense of 'one' or 'first' that the old Mishnah of Menaḥot 8:1, 3, 6 characterizes certain localities as *alpha* in semolina, *alpha* in oil, and *alpha* in wine; and it was again because the Semitic characters aleph, beth, gimel had not yet acquired numerical values that the three baskets in the Temple which were filled in a particular order and emptied in the same order (Mishnah Sheqalim, ch. 3) bore as serial marks the Greek letters alpha, beta, gamma. That the coins of the Jewish Revolts, unlike the Maccabean ones, employed numeral letters is explained by the fact that in the interim the Jews had become used to (Greek) numeral letters on the Herodian and Roman coins of Judea (Herod, of course, had merely imitated Roman models), as pointed out to me by Dr. Elias J. Bickerman. (Thus the presence of letter-numerals may legitimately be added, for good measure, to the arguments against the Maccabean dating of the 'heavy shekels.') — The two letters between the horns of the double cornucopia on some coins of Antigonus are in no case numerals; see M. Narkiss, *Maṭbe'ot 'Ereṣ Yisrael* I, 1936, p. 33; A. Reifenberg, *Ancient Jewish Coins*, 2nd ed. 1947, p. 17.

[22] In the Bethphage graffito of the Louvre, last published by E. L. Sukenik, *Tarbiz* 7 (1935/6): 102[1]–109[8]. That the one in the Franciscan museum at Jerusalem (published ibid.) is a modern forgery is argued, to my mind convincingly, by W. F. Albright, *JBL* 56 (1937): 161 nn. 46–47. But there can be no question about the authenticity of the Louvre one; see R. Dussaud, *Syria* 5 (1924): 388 f. — An excellent comprehensive paper is that of S. Gandz, Hebrew Numerals, in *Proceedings of the American Academy for Jewish Research* 4 (1932/3): 53–112, which is only slightly modified by this and the preceding footnote.

[23] So on coins of Marathus down to the year 92 B. C. E.; see B. V. Head, *Historia Numorum*, 2nd ed. 1911, pp. 792 f.

employ, to the exclusion of alphabetic numeral signs, right down to the destruction of Palmyra in 272 C. E., and their Nabatean contemporaries did likewise. [Of course we have only inscriptions by these peoples: they may have made some use of alphabet-numerals in other writings — but hardly in pre-Christian times.]

The advantage of כנשה over other words of similar formation is therefore illusory. Not so its disadvantages as compared with קהלה(א). Firstly, it is pretty obvious that it is by means of the Hebrew כנס — not קהל — that the translator has rendered the Aramaic כנש, which must have stood in his original at 2:8, 26; 3:5. Secondly, unless his original had the root *qhl* in the peal, there is no reason why the translator should, contrary to all usage, have employed this root in the qal in Hebrew. Hebrew does not employ the qal of this root at all, the correct conjugation for expressing its active meaning in that language being the hiphil. In Syriac, on the other hand, the peal of *qhl* is common and means 'to convoke,' whereas the aphel is rare and means 'to ally oneself' — which is of course inapposite. (We have to go by Syriac because the verb is not used at all in extant Jewish Aramaic sources.) In short, the perfect explanation of the Hebrew (*haq*)*Qōheleṯ* is that it is a mistranslation of an Aramaic *Qāhlā* 'the Convoker.'

13. *Ad* 10:20. The place of our במדעך was originally occupied by במרבעך 'in thy lying-place' (// 'in thy sleeping-chambers'); certainly in the Aramaic, and perhaps even in the Hebrew. (The form *marb'ā* is elsewhere — i. e. in Syriac — used of a place for *cattle* to lie in, but that is hardly a fatal objection.) Somewhere along the line, thru crowded writing and/or haplography (ב and ר being similar in appearance), the ב was lost. It will perhaps be argued that the present text is satisfactory, but that simply isn't true. It may also be argued that מרבע "could have been" used in original Hebrew composition; but the edge of such an argument quickly becomes blunted by frequent use, and the preceding paragraphs

show conclusively that Koheleth did not write in Hebrew at all.[23a]

14. An exegesis of Koh 8:1–2 which is capable of satisfying people who are not satisfied with glib solutions can be obtained with the help of the translation hypothesis and a passage in the Elephantine Aḥiqar. A series of king-gnomes in the latter reads in part as follows (ll. 101–4):

(101) חזי קדמתך מנדעם קשה [על א]נפי מ[לך] אלתקום זעיר כצפה
מן ברק אנת השתמר לך (102) אליח[וי]הי עלא[מ]ריך ותהך [ב]לא
ביומיך (103) [מל]ת מלך הן פקיד לך אשה יקדה הי עבק עבדה
[א]לתהנשק עליך ותכסה (rd. תכוה?) כפיך [(104)]ף מלת מלך
בחמר לבבא

> 'Look before thee: Something harsh (=a harsh expression) [on the f]ace of a k[ing] (means) 'Stand (=tarry) not!' His wrath is swifter than lightning: do thou take heed unto thyself that he *disp*[*lay* i]t not against thine *ut*[*tera*]*nces* and thou perish [be]fore thy time. [*Every wo*]*rd* of a king, if thou be commanded, is a burning fire. Obey at once, [le]st it be kindled upon thee and thou cover (*read* burn?) thy hands. [ ] the word of a king . . . . . .

If more people who have studied the Aḥiqar papyri intensively had taken more than a passing interest in Koheleth, or vice versa, the parallelism between the above passage and Koh 8:2–5a would have been noted long since. In addition to the general import, the following words and phrases can be seen at once to be common to both: 'a king,' 'heed,' 'stand not,' 'something harsh' ('an evil matter'), 'command(ed, -ment),' 'the word of a king.' But I think we can go a little further. V. 1 and the Elephantine parallel combined suggest very strongly that the first five letters of v. 2, which no ingenuity has yet succeeded in rendering plausibly as they stand, be emended to **אנפי** 'the face of,' and a close examination of

[23a] On a possible meaning of *mlk* in our verse, see above, Study II n. 6 and the text preceding it.

the whole of vv. 1–5a renders the emendation practically unavoidable.

In v. 1, first of all, it is best to follow the versions which take כהחכם as כה חכם. Next, חדות (or שמחת) is to be read for חכמת; or rather, חכמת is to be assumed to be original in the Hebrew, but to reflect there a חכמת which (under the influence of חכ(י)ם in the first half of the verse) had supplanted the correct חדות in the Aramaic original from which the Hebrew was made. Finally ישנא is to be vocalized *yšannē* (cf. Galling). The sense of v. 1 will then be: 'Who here is wise (*or*, is acquainted with — see immediately), and who knows the meaning of the saying "A man's pleasure lights up his face (cf. Prov 15:13 and the paradox Koh 7:3), but fierceness darkens his face (cf. Job 14:20; Lam 4:1; Dan 5:6; 7:28)"?' [Possibly, by the way, חכם misrepresents the Aramaic participle חָכֵם 'acquainted with' rather than represents the Aramaic adjective חכים 'wise.'] [See pp. 45–46 for a striking parallel from Ben Sira.]

What the proverb about whose sense he has — rhetorically — inquired means, Koheleth tells us himself by quoting another proverb, namely v. 2. Several ancient versions cited by BH[3] and followed by Ehrlich and Galling (each in his own way) rightly attach the first two words of v. 3 to the end of v. 2. At its beginning, as I have already pointed out, אנפי is to be read for אני פי. Thus the second proverb, which Koheleth cites to interpret the first, goes as follows: "Heed the face of a king, and in the matter of an oath of God be not overhasty." Whether or not the proverb, or its second clause, is of his own coining (cf. 5:1), it is only for the sake of completeness that Koheleth cites its second clause here (for a similar bit of advice on behavior vis-à-vis God and king, cf. Prov 24:21). The practical application of the observation that a man's face reflects his moods is of course contained only in the first clause, and it is only upon this that the remainder of the passage elaborates. Tho it is not essential for my purpose, it promotes coherence to change the next two words, the third and fourth in v. 3, from מפניו תלך to בפני מלך (cf. Galling). The sentence then means: 'Stand (=tarry) not in the king's presence in an evil matter (i. e. when his look is ominous)' or perhaps, in view of the Aḥiqar parallel, 'Stand (=tarry) not when there is something harsh in the king's face.' VV. 4–5 are clear.

15. Koh 10:6. 'Folly is set on great heights, while rich men sit (*or*, dwell) on low ground.' The opposite of 'folly' is 'wisdom'; not 'riches,' or — still less — 'rich men.' Conversely, the opposite of 'rich men' is 'paupers'; not 'fools,' or — still less — 'folly.' Moreover, the Hebrew words corresponding to 'is set' (*nittan*) and 'sit (*or*, dwell)' (*yēšēḇū*) are neither related to each other nor resemble one another in sound. As between 'folly' and 'rich men,' it is the former that is out of place, since the next verse shows that here the author is talking of changes in social station, not of discrimination against brains. 'Folly is set' has been able to oust an original 'the poor man sits (*or*, dwells)' thanks to the resemblance between these two phrases in Aramaic; where the former is יהיב סכלא and the latter — the original reading — ית(י)ב מסכנא. (יְתֵב, יָתֵב, and יְתִיב are all equally good Aramaic.) The Hebrew for the latter would be — in the style of our translator — ישב המסכן.

16. I should further mention that it is at least possible that in Koh 4:8 — as certainly in Dan 10:13, 20[24] — אני 'I' renders an Aramaic אנה which the translator either found or misread in his *vorlage* where the author in *his* copy had written, or at least intended to write, דנה 'this one'; while in Koh 5:3 *ḥpṣ* is not improbably to be vocalized *ḥāpēṣ* (participle), so that אין חפץ will be inferior Hebrew for איננו חפץ and analogous to אין נוגע in Dan 8:5 (and perhaps to אין מבין in Dan 8:27).[25] That is to say, the translator, having before him לא צָבֵה 'He (God) takes no pleasure' remembered that negation of the participle in Hebrew is, except in certain

[24] *SD* 60–61.
[25] Ibid. 57–8.

cases, effected by means of אין, but did not remember that if the subject is not otherwise expressed the appropriate pronominal suffix must be added to this אין.

17. I have already made suggestions in Study I on Koh 2:12,[26] 26.[27]

What becomes, in the light of the foregoing, of most of the arguments of the opposition — that just translations are always smooth, that a translator doesn't translate the same phrase once correctly and once otherwise; that no translator could have been capable of such "stupidity"; that this, that, and the other semantic development "could have" taken place in Hebrew; or this or that bit of erratic grammar "could" be explained by special circumstances; and so on?[28] When an *a posteriori* reasoning from inductions leads inescapably to deductions which are diametrically opposed to inferences made from *a priori* considerations, either the latter conclusions are non sequiturs or the premises from which they flow are themselves unsound. There is probably not a single phenomenon alleged by Zimmermann and me which can not be paralleled in the Septuagint. I have already adduced parallels from the LXX renderings of Koheleth and other books to the non-use and misuse of the article in the translation-Hebrew of Koheleth. It would perhaps not be fair to cite any more from the LXX to Koheleth itself; which, being executed in accordance with the principles of Aquila, is deliberately barbaric, and offers the most startling contrast imaginable to the stylistic excellence of the English translation

[26] See above, Study I n. 11.

[27] Ibid. n. 16.

[28] Following this mode of reasoning, TTQR concludes (p. 116): "As for the theory that the Hebrew Qohelet is a translation of a non-existent Aramaic original, it may be said, *quod demonstrandum erat etiam-nunc demonstrandum est.*" But for that matter Eduardus Boehl, *De Aramaismis Libri Koheleth*, Erlangae MDCCCLX, arrived, in much the same manner, at the verdict (p. 45): "Non igitur Aramaismos in Ecclesiasta recentioris quam Salomonis aetatis indicia esse dixerim."

in *WK*. I shall, however, continue to stress the LXX to the other parts of the Bible. It has been claimed that the very inelegances of the Hebrew of Koheleth argue for its originality, in view of the appreciably inferior smoothness of the Hebrew of Hosea as compared with that of modern English versions. The weakness of that argument has been pointed out by Zimmermann, and a comparison of the Hebrew of Hosea with the Septuagint would be much more to the point. Here articles are omitted tho needed, if the corresponding Hebrew substantives happen to be in the construct state (or to govern pronominal suffixes, which is merely a special case of the same thing),[29] and monstrosities like *ekporneuousa ekporneusei* (1:2) *antitassomenos antitaxomai* (1:6), and *dioti theos egō eimi kai ouk anthrōpos* (11:9) are indulged in. (This last could only mean: For it is I, not man, who am a God; whereas the sense required is: For I am a God, not a man. The Greek sentence would have this sense were it not for the word *egō*, but the Greek translators express by a special word nearly every pronoun or pronominal suffix which they find — or, in some instances, fancy they find — in the Hebrew.) One also finds such howlers as 'locust' for 'lattice' (both are spelled *'rbh* in Hebrew, but the context — Hos 13:3 — would be an ample guide to (1) a trained scholar equipped with (2) a lexicon and (3) a concordance and — something whose absolute non-existence prior to the invention of the codex ought not to need the stressing it does — (4) a Bible both complete and easy to handle), just as one finds 'tortoises' for 'stone-heaps' (the former signification would be possible per se, as in Sifra Shemini V 4; but again look at the context, Hos 12:12). In spite of all that, the translator in question did not succeed in ruining entirely Hos 14:2 ff.; which goes to show how feeble an argument against the translation hypothesis in Koheleth is the impressiveness of Koh 12:1 ff. (Which I am sure was even more impressive, because more intelligible, in the Aramaic

[29] See above, para. 6.

original.) Anybody who has some knowledge of both Hebrew and Greek and a considerable knowledge of one of them has only to read from ten to twenty chapters of Septuagint to discover for himself plenty of further illustrations of the sort of thing Zimmermann and I impute to the Hebrew translator of Koheleth. That applies even to the comparatively smooth rendering of Genesis, let alone the barbaric jargon of the Greek Judges. There are, of course, some books on the subject; and Zimmermann, QHQ 80 n. 2, cites a couple. I further recommend the introduction to Connybeare and Stock, *Selections from the Septuagint*, 1905, pp. 1–100. And since the translation of Koheleth from Aramaic into Hebrew may have been executed nearly simultaneously with that of Ben Sira from Hebrew into Greek (132 B.C.E. or a few years later) — see below pp. 44–45 — the evaluation of the latter by Israel Lévi, *L'Ecclésiastique* I, 1898, pp. XL–XLV, also makes rather interesting reading.

Nor is there any cogency to the argument that Zimmermann's hesitation about the particular dialect of Aramaic in which the original was composed speaks against its having been composed in any dialect of Aramaic. The fact is that the features which can be discerned thru the veil of the Hebrew version are mostly common Aramaic ones. By the same token, it will not be regarded by any serious scholar as a fresh argument against the translation hypothesis that concerning the precise variety of Aramaic underlying the Hebrew there is also a difference of opinion between Zimmermann and me. I too am hesitant, but the balance of internal and external evidence seems to me to favor something very much like the Aramaic of Daniel. However, the alternative to that as the original language of Koheleth is not Koheleth-Hebrew but some other variety of Aramaic.

IV

DATES OF COMPOSITION AND TRANSLATION

Once the Hebrew of Koheleth has been proved to be a translation (Study III), it can no longer serve in the same manner as formerly either as a source for the history of the Hebrew language or as a criterion for determining the date of the book's composition. Indeed, it is of only limited helpfulness for dating the translation, since most of its characteristic features would be equally remarkable for any age and equally liable to occur in Hebrew translated from Aramaic in any age. Nevertheless the language does furnish a few clues to both the period of the author and that of the translator.

(1) Thus *pardēs* (2:5) and *piṯḡām* (8:11) are both Persian loanwords,[1] and consequently could not be employed either in the Aramaic original or in the Hebrew translation before the *late sixth* century. (2) *'ḏen(ā)* (4:2, 3), which is contracted from *'aḏ hēnnā* (Gen 15:16; etc.), is specifically Hebrew, and therefore reflects only the date of translation, not that of composition. It otherwise occurs[1a] only in post-biblical Hebrew, the latest other biblical passages where it might have been used, 1 Chr 9:18; 12:30, having still the uncontracted expression; so that it can hardly have arisen before the *fourth* century. (3) *'Illū* (6:6), finally, being an Aramaic loanword composed of the two elements *'en* 'if' (non-committal as to whether the condition actually obtains) and *lū* (cf. Heb., Arab.,

[1] That *piṯḡām* is not the Greek *phthegma* or *epitagma* has been finally proved by its occurrence in the Persian phrase *gst ptgm* 'something evil' in an Aramaic leather scroll of the fifth century. See Polotsky and Kutsher, *Kedem* 2 (1945): 66–74.

[1a] In the form *'ḏain.*

Accad.) 'if' (implying that in fact the condition does not obtain), can not have arisen in Aramaic before the *third* century, since the first of these elements was originally *hen* and is still *hen* in Daniel A (Dan 1–6), which is to be dated about 304 B. C. E. (see further on). (No example occurs in Daniel B.)

A dating in the late fourth or in the third century is further suggested by the very fact that the author wrote in Aramaic. The plain sense of Neh 13:23–24 is that in the governorship of Nehemiah (ca. 430 B. C. E.) inability to speak Hebrew was exceptional in Judah, and that the half-Jews among whom it was encountered did not speak, in its stead, Aramaic but dialects more or less akin to Hebrew. It is true that Aramaization proceeded more rapidly in Jerusalem (which among other things kept absorbing fresh arrivals from the diaspora) than in some other parts of the country (since western Judah seems from various indications to have remained at least partly Hebrew-speaking well into the Roman age); but even so, surely at least two generations had to elapse from the time of Nehemiah before a Jew in Jerusalem — the view that the author of Koh 1:12; 2:7b, 9a was a diaspora Jew must be supported by very strong positive indications to be taken seriously — could decide to compose a book of 'gems of expression' (דברי חפץ, 12:10) in Aramaic. Even four or five generations after Nehemiah, a traditionalist and specialist in Scripture like Ben Sira wrote in Hebrew.

Another early Jewish book which was certainly composed in Aramaic and which there is every reason for believing to have been composed, in its present form, in Palestine is Daniel A (Dan 1–6). This I formerly dated in the first half of the third century, but I indicated that I should have dated it ca. 304 were it not for the expression *mārē molḵīn* 'Lord of kingships' in Dan 2:47.[2] However, it has since come to light that the pharaonic title *nb.tj* was thus

[2] See my *Studies in Daniel*, pp. 7–8.

rendered in Aramaic by Asiatics as early as ca. 600 B. C. E.,[3] and it may consequently have been somehow preserved by them during the centuries between the brief Saitic and the long Ptolemaic sovereignty over territories in western Asia. Its preservation, as Professor Albrecht Alt suggests in a letter of the 13th of August, 1949, may have been aided by the fact that the Achaemenid kings, in their quality of kings of Egypt, were also Pharaohs. I therefore now favor more the dating ca. 304 for Daniel A; and since *'illū*, as we have seen, points to a later date than that of Daniel A (unless the translator has modernized a **hinlu* or **hillu* in his original), Koheleth can not date from earlier than the third century B. C. E.

This dating receives some slight confirmation from the sense in which the author uses the word *pardēs* (2:5), namely '(economically productive) orchard.' The Greek *paradeisos* did not acquire this signification until the third century;[4] and it is doubtful if this sense may be ascribed to *pardēs* in Canticles, where it may mean rather 'pleasure-garden' (Cant 4:13), with the emphasis on the etymological sense of 'enclosure' (4:12). Certainly in Neh 2:8 (fifth century) the word means the same thing as in Xenophon: 'game-preserve.'

This about exhausts the purely linguistic evidence, since recent observations[5] have raised as much doubt about the Greek provenience of 'under the sun' in the Eshmunazorid inscriptions and Koheleth as about the Greek provenience of 'lord of kingships' in the Eshmunazorid inscriptions and Daniel 2:47.

[3] Published by A. Dupont-Sommer, *Semitica* 1 (1948): 43–68, with photograph. Further observations by H. L. Ginsberg, *BASOR* 111 (Oct. 1948): 24–27; A. Malamat, *BJPES* 15 (1949): 34–39.

[4] Very reminiscent of Koh 2:4–5 is a decree (Papyrus Petrie III, 26) to the effect that "if an ox, or beast of burden, or sheep, or any other animal, trespass on another man's arable land, or orchard (*paradeison*), or garden (*kēpon*), or vineyard (*ampelōna*)," the owner of that animal is liable etc. (Reference due to Dr. Bickerman.)

[5] See J. Friedrich, *Orientalia* NS 18 (1949): 15–29.

As for other indications, Ben Sira's dependence upon Koheleth can hardly be questioned,[6] so that 190–180 can serve as a *terminus ante quem*. Otherwise, of Koheleth's two polemics — against belief in the immortality of the individual, and against senseless toiling to amass wealth for its own sake instead of for use and to the extent that one can use it (I A 8) — the first, tho conceivable in any age, is particularly understandable in the third century B. C. E., when belief in a real afterlife was beginning to gain considerable adherence in Jewry, and indeed in the form of a polemic against the peculiarly Platonic notion that the human soul as such 'goes upward' (is immortal because it is divine) — Koh 3:18–21 — it could not very well be understood in any other age; while the second, as Dr. Bickerman has pointed out to me, fits perfectly into just this period. For not only does Ben Sira voice the same sentiments (Ben Sira 14:11–[17])[7] — apparently not independently of Koheleth — but both Ben Sira (34 [31]:1–4) and pagan writers from 300 B. C. E. on stress the limitations of wealth in complete independence of Koheleth. Thus Menander (ca. 300), Fragment 128 K, declares: "Money is an insecure thing. It belongs not to you but to Fortune. She may give it to somebody else who is unworthy." And in Fragment 281 K: "I used to think the wealthy did not groan or toss up and down in the night but enjoyed slumber. But now I see that you, the so-called happy ones, suffer like us." Again, Metrodorus, a disciple of Epicurus (likewise fl. 300), is stated by Philodemus, *Oeconomica* 18, to have written that it is good to acquire wealth 'provided one does not get more trouble from it than pleasure' (*hōste mē pleiō ponein dia ta khrēmata ēper eupathein*).[8] On the other

[6] So, after a cautious appraisal of the linguistic evidence, Th. Nöldeke, *ZAW* 20 (1900): 90–92. — Except that he wrongly dispenses with all reservations vis-à-vis the Genizah Hebrew text of Ben-Sira, Barton, pp. 54–56, presents the complete data on Ben Sira's debt of ideas and diction to Koheleth in an admirable and convincing manner.

[7] Cf. above, I n. 2a.

[8] Cf., e. g., Koh 5:11 ff.

hand, Koheleth's bitter observation that the man who lacks worldly goods is not listened to tho he possess wisdom (Koh 9:13–16b) is likewise echoed not only by Ben Sira (13:22 [26]–[29]) but also by Menander, Fr. 856 K, "A poor man is not believed even when he speaks the truth," and by his contemporary Philemon, Fr. 102 K, "Even if he begins like a sage and says something sensible, the poor man seems to be talking badly to those who hear him." These ideas then become commonplaces of the popular moralizing philosophy of the Hellenistic age. For the "American" type of the restless selfmade man who is too busy making money to stop to enjoy it is, like the opportunities for his rise, a product of the Hellenistic period; and so, it would seem, is the popular worship of success and the contempt, bordering on hatred, of the rich for the needy (Ben Sira 13:20 [24]). They were as much of a novelty in Greece as in the Orient. The glorification of youth over age (Koh 11:9—12:5), on the other hand, is something new for the East, but not for Hellas; which had always idolized the naked ephebes exercising in the *palaistra*. So too misogyny makes its appearance in Israel with Koheleth (7:28) and Ben Sira (7:24–25; 25:13 ff.; 42:6, 9–14), but among the Greeks it can be traced back to the fifth century B. C. E. (Euripides, Aristophanes) and even to the sixth (Simonides).[9–10]

A third century date for Koheleth, which has long been generally favored, therefore seems to be indicated strongly by some circumstances and at least to fit in well with others. For his translator, only the Maccabean age enters into consideration. There is no other period subsequent to the third century B. C. E. when an Aramaic work was likely both to be translated into Hebrew and

[9] Cf. I. Lévi, *L'Ecclesiastique* II, 1901, pp. LXII–LXIV.

[10] For a suggested explanation of the appearance of misogyny in Israel just in the third and second centuries, and for a fuller and more competent discussion of Koheleth in the light of contemporary history, see Bickerman's forthcoming history of the Jews in the Hellenistic period.

to become canonical. In that era of national revival, on the other hand, both things are known to have happened to the first and to the last five chapters of the book of Daniel.

Addendum to p. 35

Ben Sira 13:25–26 goes like this:

(25) *A man's heart will change his visage*
either for better or worse.
(26) *A sign of a glad heart's a bright face;*
and . . . .

The first three lines alone express so exactly the idea of Koh 8:1 as I have reconstructed it — "A man's pleasure lights up his face, but fierceness darkens his face" — as to add plausibility to that reconstruction.

It is legitimate to emphasize firstly that the said reconstruction is abundantly plausible without this support, and secondly — and more particularly — that this support is in no way dependent upon any exegesis or reconstruction of the fourth line of Ben Sira's dictum. On the contrary, it is my reconstruction of the verse in Koheleth that suggests a restoration of the fourth line of the passage in Ben Sira: one which, so far as my interpretation of Koh 8:1 is concerned, the reader may take or leave. However, he will enjoy p. 35 the more for taking *all* of pp. 45–46.

The wording, then, of Ben Sira 13:26b in the Genizah Hebrew text is for once, on the one hand, such as possibly *could* have given rise to the widely divergent (but equally insipid) renderings in the Greek and the Syriac and, on the other, can not readily be explained as a retranslation of either (tho it too is suspect). It reads: ושיג ושיח מחשבת עמל. So far as I can see, no philologically permissible rendering of that can differ very much from the following: 'but care and sorrow[1] are anguished thought.'[2] Yet such

[1] שיח is known to have some such meaning in 1 Sam 1:16; Ps 55:3; etc.; and whoever is responsible for our Hebrew Ben Sira would seem to have assumed, perhaps rightly, that in 1 Ki 18:27 both שיח and its parallel sequent שיג mean 'care,' or 'distraction.'

[2] This rendering takes *'āmāl* in the sense of 'suffering' (Ps 73:5; Job 11:16; etc.). 'Wicked scheming' would also be possible per se, but it would not fit into the context.

a truism suits the context little better than either of the versions. I consequently surmise that the last word in the Hebrew was originally עינ(ים) 'eye(s),'[3] and the last word but one some derivative of ־חשכ־ 'to be dark' rather than of ־חשב־ 'to think.' For a line like

ושיג ושיח (מ)חשכ(ת) עינ(ים)

would be rather attractive Hebrew for

and of care and sorrow,[4] *dull-ey'dness.*[5]

Which speaks for itself.

[3] The Peshitta's 'sinners' (according to the diacritical marks, *plural*) could have arisen from this — misread עונ(י)ם and connected by the translator with '*āwōn* — at least as easily as from עמל; and that even the younger Siracide's 'labor' may go back to עי/ונ(י)ם, taken as equivalent to אונ(י)ם, is suggested by the fact that the Septuagint regularly renders און by one or other of the Greek words meaning 'labor, toil.' Indeed, to take עי/ונ(י)ם as equivalent to אונ(י)ם was almost the only course open to the Greek translator of Ben Sira 13:26b once the ־חשכ־ of the preceding word was confused with ־חשב־; cf. *dialogismoi meta kopou* here with *dialogismoi ponōn sou* (<מחשבות אונך) in Jer 4:14 LXX and with *logizomenoi kopous* (<חשבי און) in Micah 2:1 LXX. — *If* that is what happened, מחשבת עמל in our Hebrew text is not simply a scribal corruption of the original (מ)חשכ(ת) עינ(י)ם but is a retroversion from the Greek or from some daughter-version of the Greek. In other passages, it is almost impossible to escape the conclusion that the extant Hebrew goes back directly or indirectly to the Greek, notably 25:17 (Heb. 16). Here, firstly, only 'it darkens his face like sackcloth' really makes sense. The biblical sackcloth is a fabric woven of goats' hair, and is of the same dark hue as the goats from which it is derived or the bedouin tents which are — to this day — made of it. (Most Oriental goats are black or brown.) If therefore it is natural to compare dark objects to goats (Cant 4:1b; 6:5b) or to bedouin tents (Cant 1:5), it is equally natural to compare them to sackcloth (Isa 50:3). Secondly, 'like sackcloth' is what both the Peshitta and two Greek uncials have (*hōs sakkon*). And thirdly, the other Greek codices have the surely corrupt 'like a bear' (*hōs arkos*), from which our Hebrew (לדוב) would seem to be translated as surely (and as directly?) as the Syriac of the Syrohexaplar version or the Latin of the Vulgate. This is one of the many problems in Ben Sira that await competent investigation. [In passing, the first half of the same verse, Ben Sira 25:17 (Heb. 16), contains another example of the idiom 'to change (=to darken) the look.' The Hebrew original of the Greek's *alloioi* was perhaps ישנה, hardly (as in our Hebrew text) ישחיר.]

[4] I. e., 'and a sign of care and sorrow is etc.' No explanation is needed when one reads this line together with the first half of the verse, thus: *A sign of a glad heart's a bright face; / and of care and sorrow, dull-ey'dness. //*

[5] Cf. Ps 6:8; Job 17:7; Deut 28:65 (where the Peshitta renders by means of חשכא דעינא and the Jewish Targums similarly); etc.

Date Due

